THE DALAI LAMA'S BOOK OF LOVE AND COMPASSION

The DALAI LAMA'S *Book of* LOVE AND COMPASSION

HIS HOLINESS THE DALAI LAMA

Thorsons

Thorsons
An Imprint of HarperCollins*Publishers*
77–85 Fulham Palace Road,
Hammersmith, London W6 8JB

The website address is: www.thorsonselement.com

Material for this book previously published in
The Four Noble Truths
The Power of Compassion

The text is taken from a talk given by His Holiness the Dalai Lama at the Free Trade Hall in Manchester, England, on July 19, 1996, and questions and answers from a series of lectures by His Holiness.

Published by Thorsons 2001

2 4 6 8 10 9 7 5 3 1

A catalogue record for this book is available from the British Library

ISBN-13 978-0-00-743524-1

Printed and bound in India by
Thomson Press India Ltd.

CONTENTS

COMPASSION: THE BASIS FOR HUMAN HAPPINESS

I think that every human being has an innate sense of "I." We cannot explain why that feeling is there, but it is. Along with it comes a desire for happiness and a wish to overcome suffering. This is quite justified: we have a natural right to achieve as much happiness as possible, and we also have the right to overcome suffering.

The whole of human history has developed on the basis of this feeling. In fact it is not limited to human beings; from the Buddhist point of view, even the tiniest insect has this feeling and, according to its capacity, is trying to gain some happiness and avoid unhappy situations.

However, there are some major differences between human beings and other animal species. They stem from human intelligence. On account of our intelligence, we are much more advanced and have a greater capacity. We are able to think much farther into the future, and our memory is powerful enough to take us back many years. Furthermore, we have oral and written traditions which remind us of events many centuries ago. Now, thanks to scientific methods, we can even examine events which occurred millions of years ago.

~

So our intelligence makes us very smart, but at the same time, precisely because of that fact, we also have more doubts and suspicions, and hence more fears. I think the imagination of fear is much more developed in humans than in other animals. In addition, the many conflicts within the human family and within one's own family, not to mention the conflicts within the community and between nations, as well as the internal conflicts within the individual – all conflicts and contradictions arise from the different ideas and views our intelligence brings. So unfortunately, intelligence can sometimes create a quite unhappy state of mind. In this sense, it becomes another source of human misery. Yet, at the same time, I think that, ultimately, intelligence is the tool with which we can overcome all these conflicts and differences.

From this point of view, of all the various species of animal on the planet, human beings are the biggest troublemakers. That is clear. I imagine that if there were no longer any humans on the planet, the planet itself would be safer! Certainly millions of fish, chicken, and other small animals might enjoy some sort of genuine liberation!

It is therefore important that human intelligence be utilized in a constructive way. That is the key. If we utilize its capacity properly, then not only human beings would become less harmful to each other, and to the planet, but also individual human beings would be happier in themselves. It is in our hands. Whether we utilize our intelligence in the right way or the wrong way is up to us. Nobody can impose their values on us. How can we learn to use our capacity constructively? First, we need to recognize our nature and then, if we have the determination, there is a real possibility of transforming the human heart.

On this basis, I will speak on how a human being can find happiness as an individual, because I believe the individual is the key to all the rest. For change to happen in any community, the initiative must come from the individual. If the individual can become a good, calm, peaceful person, this automatically brings a positive atmosphere to the family around him or her. When parents are warm-hearted, peaceful and calm people, generally speaking their children will also develop that attitude and behavior.

The way our attitude works is such that it is often troubled by outside factors, so one side of the issue is to eliminate the existence of trouble around you. The environment, meaning the surrounding situation, is a very important factor for establishing a happy frame of mind. However, even more important is the other side of the issue, which is one's own mental attitude.

~

The surrounding situation may not be so friendly, it may even be hostile, but if your inner mental attitude is right, then the situation will not disturb your inner peace. On the other hand, if your attitude is not right, then even if you are surrounded by good friends and the best facilities, you cannot be happy. This is why mental attitude is more important than external conditions. Despite this, it seems to me that many people are more concerned about their external conditions, and neglect the inner attitude of mind. I suggest that we should pay more attention to our inner qualities.

There are a number of qualities which are important for mental peace, but from the little experience I have, I believe that one of the most important factors is human compassion and affection: a sense of caring.

~

Let me explain what we mean by compassion. Usually, our concept of compassion or love refers to the feeling of closeness we have with our friends and loved ones. Sometimes compassion also carries a sense of pity. This is wrong – any love or compassion which entails looking down on the other is not genuine compassion. To be genuine, compassion must be based on respect for the other, and on the realization that others have the right to be happy and overcome suffering just as much as you. On this basis, since you can see that others are suffering, you develop a genuine sense of concern for them.

As for the closeness we feel toward our friends, this is usually more like attachment than compassion. Genuine compassion should be unbiased. If we only feel close to our friends, and not to our enemies, or to the countless people who are unknown to us personally and toward whom we are indifferent, then our compassion is only partial or biased.

As I mentioned before, genuine compassion is based on the recognition that others have the right to happiness just like yourself, and therefore even your enemy is a human being with the same wish for happiness as you, and the same right to happiness as you. A sense of concern developed on this basis is what we call compassion; it extends to everyone, irrespective of whether the person's attitude toward you is hostile or friendly.

One aspect of this kind of compassion is a sense of caring responsibility. When we develop that kind of motivation, our self-confidence increases automatically. This in turn reduces fear, and that serves as a basis for determination. If you are really determined right from the beginning to accomplish a difficult task, then even if you fail first time, second time, third time, it doesn't matter. Your aim is very clear, so you will continue to make an effort. This sort of optimistic and determined attitude is a key factor for success.

Compassion also brings us an inner strength. Once it is developed, it naturally opens an inner door, through which we can communicate with fellow human beings, and even other sentient beings, with ease, and heart to heart. On the other hand, if you feel hatred and ill-feeling toward others, they may feel similarly toward you, and as a result suspicion and fear will create a distance between you and make communication difficult. You will then feel lonely and isolated. Not all members of your community will have similar negative feelings toward you, but some may look on you negatively because of your own feeling.

~

If you harbor negative feelings toward others, and yet expect them to be friendly to you, you are being illogical. If you want the atmosphere around you to be more friendly, you must first create the basis for that. Whether the response of others is positive or negative, you must first create the ground of friendliness. If others still respond to you negatively after this, then you have the right to act accordingly.

~

I always try to create a ground of friendliness with people. Whenever I meet someone new, for example, I feel no need for introductions. The person is obviously another human being. Maybe sometime in the future, technological advances may mean that I could confuse a robot for a human being, but up to now this has never happened. I see a smile, some teeth and eyes, and so on, and I recognize the person as a human being! On that basis, on the emotional level we are the same, and basically on the physical level we are the same, except for coloring. But whether Westerners have yellow hair, or blue hair, or white hair, does not really matter. The important thing is that we are the same on the emotional level. With that conviction, I feel that the other person is a human brother, and approach him spontaneously. In most cases, the other person immediately responds accordingly, and becomes a friend. Sometimes I fail, and then I have the liberty to react according to the circumstances.

Basically, therefore, we should approach others openly, recognizing each person as another human being just like ourselves. There is not so much difference between us all.

Compassion naturally creates a positive atmosphere, and as a result you feel peaceful and content. Wherever there lives a compassionate person, there is always a pleasant atmosphere. Even dogs and birds approach the person easily. Almost fifty years ago, I used to keep some birds in the Norbulingka Summer Palace, in Lhasa. Among them was a small parrot. At that time I had an elderly attendant whose appearance was somewhat unfriendly – he had very round, stern eyes – but he was always feeding this parrot with nuts and so on. So whenever the attendant would appear, just the sound of his footsteps or his coughing would mean the parrot would show some excitement. The attendant had an extraordinarily friendly manner with that small bird, and the parrot also had an amazing response to him. On a few occasions I fed him some nuts but he never showed such friendliness to me, so I started to poke him with a stick, hoping he might react differently; the result was totally negative. I was using more force than the bird had, so it reacted accordingly.

Therefore, if you want a genuine friend, first you must create a positive atmosphere around you. We are social animals, after all, and friends are very important. How can you bring a smile to people's faces? If you remain stony and suspicious, it is very difficult. Perhaps if you have power or money, some people may offer you an artificial smile, but a genuine smile will only come from compassion.

The question is how to develop compassion. In fact, can we really develop unbiased compassion at all? My answer is that we definitely can. I believe that human nature is gentle and compassionate, although many people, in the past and now, think that it is basically aggressive. Let us examine this point.

~

At the time of conception, and while we are in our mother's womb, our mother's compassionate and peaceful mental state is a very positive factor for our development. If the mother's mind is very agitated, it is harmful for us. And that is just the beginning of life! Even the parents' state of mind at conception is important. If a child is conceived through rape, for example, then it will be unwanted, which is a terrible thing. For conception to take place properly, it should come from genuine love and mutual respect, not just mad passion. It is not enough to have some casual love affair, the two partners should know each other well and respect each other as people; this is the basis for a happy marriage. Furthermore, marriage itself should be for life, or at least should be long lasting. Life should properly start from such a situation.

Then, according to medical science, in the few weeks after birth, the child's brain is still growing. During that period, the experts claim that physical touch is a crucial factor for the proper development of the brain. This alone shows that the mere growth of our body requires another's affection.

~

After birth, one of the first acts on the mother's side is to give milk, and from the child's side it is to suckle. Milk is often considered a symbol of compassion. Without it, traditionally the child cannot survive. Through the process of suckling there comes a closeness between mother and child. If that closeness is not there, then the child will not seek its mother's breast, and if the mother is feeling dislike toward the child her milk may not come freely. So milk comes with affection. This means that the first act of our life, that of taking milk, is a symbol of affection.

It has been found that those children who grow up in homes where there is love and affection have a healthier physical development and study better at school. Conversely, those who lack human affection have more difficulty in developing physically and mentally. These children also find it difficult to show affection when they grow up, which is such a great tragedy.

Now let us look at the last moment of our lives – death. Even at the time of death, although the dying person can no longer benefit much from his friends, if he is surrounded by friends his mind may be more calm. Therefore throughout our lives, from the very beginning right up to our death, human affection plays a very important role.

An affectionate disposition not only makes the mind more peaceful and calm, but it affects our body in a positive way too. On the other hand, hatred, jealousy and fear upset our peace of mind, make us agitated and affect our body adversely. Even our body needs peace of mind, and is not suited to agitation. This shows that an appreciation of peace of mind is in our blood.

Therefore, although some may disagree, I feel that although the aggressive side of our nature is part of life, the dominant force of life is human affection. This is why it is possible to strengthen that basic goodness which is our human nature.

~

We can also approach the importance of compassion through intelligent reasoning. If I help another person, and show concern for him or her, then I myself will benefit from that. However, if I harm others, eventually I will be in trouble. I often joke, half sincerely and half seriously, saying that if we wish to be truly selfish then we should be wisely selfish rather than foolishly selfish. Our intelligence can help to adjust our attitude in this respect. If we use it well, we can gain insight as to how we can fulfill our own self-interest by leading a compassionate way of life.

In this context, I do not think that selfishness is wrong. Loving oneself is crucial. If we do not love ourselves, how can we love others? It seems that when some people talk of compassion, they have the notion that it entails a total disregard for one's own interests – a sacrificing of one's interests. This is not the case. In fact genuine love should first be directed at oneself.

There are two different senses of self. One has no hesitation in harming other people, and that is negative and leads to trouble. The other is based on determination, willpower, and self-confidence, and that sense of "I" is very necessary. Without it, how can we develop the confidence we need to carry out any task in life? Similarly, there are two types of desire also. However, hatred is invariably negative and destructive of harmony.

~

How can we reduce hatred? Hatred is usually preceded by anger. Anger rises as a reactive emotion, and gradually develops into a feeling of hatred. The skillful approach here is first to know that anger is negative. Often people think that as anger is part of us, it is better to express it, but I think this is misguided. You may have grievances or resentment due to your past, and by expressing your anger you might be able to finish with them. That is very possible. Usually, however, it is better to check your anger, and then gradually, year by year, it diminishes. In my experience, this works best when you adopt the position that anger is negative and it is better not to feel it. That position itself will make a difference.

Whenever anger is about to come, you can train yourself to see the object of your anger in a different light. Any person or circumstance which causes anger is basically relative; seen from one angle it makes you angry, but seen from another perspective you may discover some good things in it. We lost our country, for example, and became refugees. If we look at our situation from that angle, we might feel frustration and sadness, yet the same event has created new opportunities – meeting with other people from different religious traditions, and so on. Developing a more flexible way of seeing things helps

~

us cultivate a more balanced mental attitude. This is one method.

~

~

There are other situations where you might fall sick, for example, and the more you think about your sickness the worse your frustration becomes. In such a case, it is very helpful to compare your situation with the worst case scenario related to your illness, or with what would have happened if you had caught an even more serious illness, and so on. In this way, you can console yourself by realizing that it could have been much worse. Here again, you train yourself to see the relativity of your situation. If you compare it with something that is much worse, this will immediately reduce your frustration.

~

Similarly, if difficulties come they may appear enormous when you look at them closely, but if you approach the same problem from a wider perspective, it appears smaller. With these methods, and by developing a larger outlook, you can reduce your frustration whenever you face problems. You can see that constant effort is needed, but if you apply it in this way, then the angry side of you will diminish. Meanwhile, you strengthen your compassionate side and increase your good potential. By combining these two approaches, a negative person can be transformed into a kind one.

~

In addition, if you have religious faith, it can be useful in extending these qualities. For example, the Gospels teach us to turn the other cheek, which clearly shows the practice of tolerance. For me, the main message of the Gospels is love for our fellow human beings, and the reason we should develop this is because we love God. I understand this in the sense of having infinite love. Such religious teachings are very powerful to increase and extend our good qualities. The Buddhist approach presents a very clear method. First, we try to consider all sentient beings as equal. Then we consider that the lives of all beings are just as precious as our own, and through this we develop a sense of concern for others.

~

What of the case of someone who has no religious faith? Whether we follow a religion or not is a matter of individual right. It is possible to manage without religion, and in some cases it may make life simpler! But when you no longer have any interest in religion, you should not neglect the value of good human qualities. As long as we are human beings, and members of human society, we need human compassion. Without that, you cannot be happy. Since we all want to be happy, and to have a happy family and friends, we have to develop compassion and affection. It is important to recognize that there are two levels of

~

spirituality, one with religious faith, and one without. With the latter, we simply try to be a warm-hearted person.

~

We should also remember that once we cultivate a compassionate attitude, non-violence comes automatically. Non-violence is not a diplomatic word, it is compassion in action. If you have hatred in your heart, then very often your actions will be violent, whereas if you have compassion in your heart, your actions will be non-violent.

~

As I said earlier, as long as human beings remain on this Earth there will always be disagreements and conflicting views. We can take that as given. If we use violence in order to reduce disagreements and conflict, then we must expect violence every day and I think the result of this is terrible. Furthermore, it is actually impossible to eliminate disagreements through violence. Violence only brings even more resentment and dissatisfaction.

~

~

Non-violence, on the other hand, means dialogue, it means using language to communicate. And dialogue means compromise: listening to others' views, and respecting others' rights, in a spirit of reconciliation. Nobody will be a 100 percent winner, and nobody will be a 100 percent loser. That is the practical way. In fact, that is the only way. Today, as the world becomes smaller and smaller, the concept of "us" and "them" is almost out-dated. If our interests existed independently of those of others, then it would be possible to have a complete winner and a complete loser, but since in reality we all depend on one another,

~

our interests and those of others are very interconnected. So how can you gain a 100 percent victory? It is impossible. You have to share, half-half, or maybe 60 percent this side and 40 percent the other side! Without this approach, reconciliation is impossible.

~

~

The reality of the world today means that we need to learn to think in this way. This is the basis of my own approach – the "middle way" approach. Tibetans will not be able to gain 100 percent victory because whether we like it or not, the future of Tibet very much depends on China. Therefore, in the spirit of reconciliation, I advocate a sharing of interests so that genuine progress is possible. Compromise is the only way. Through non-violent means we can share views, feelings, and rights, and in this way we can solve the problem.

~

I sometimes call the 20th century a century of bloodshed, a century of war. Over this century there have been more conflicts, more bloodshed, and more weapons than ever before. Now, on the basis of the experience we have all had in this century, and of what we have learned from it, I think we should look to the next century to be one of dialogue. The principle of non-violence should be practiced everywhere. This cannot be achieved simply by sitting here and praying. It means work and effort, and yet more effort.

QUESTIONS AND ANSWERS

Your Holiness, in this modern world, we try to avoid suffering. This only seems to create more suffering in that one person's positive work can be someone else's suffering, for instance medicine, politics, and so on. How do we judge? Shouldn't we just accept a certain amount of suffering and discomfort?

I think that there are many levels of suffering. Generally speaking, it is definitely possible to reduce the level of suffering. I don't personally believe that conditions that are essential for one's wellbeing and happiness necessarily involve harming and affecting someone else's life in a negative way.

Here I would like to say something. I feel that television and newspapers usually report negative things. Killings, for example, or unfortunate events are immediately reported. In the meantime, millions of people are actually receiving help, or being nourished or looked after by human affection, such as millions of children, sick and old people. But usually in people's minds these good things are taken for granted. They are not seen as something to which we should pay special attention. Actually, this shows that the very nature of humanity is compassion or affection. We simply ignore all the work of affection because it seems natural. But we are surprised at things like bloodshed; it shocks our minds because our nature is not of that kind.

As a result, many people get the impression that human nature is negative, aggressive, and

~

violent. I think that psychologically this is very bad, especially for young children who, through television, see negative human elements, but always for a short time. At that moment or for a short period, these things like killing or hitting can be a little bit exciting. But in the long-term, I think these violent things are very, very harmful to society. In fact, I recently had a meeting with Karl Popper, the philosopher. We have known each other since 1973. In our meeting we discussed violence on television and my view that too much violence is having a very negative impact on the minds of millions of children. He is, I think, of the same opinion. A proper way of education is the most important element in terms of hope for a better future.

Your Holiness, what is your answer on how to stop pollution in the universe? Will there have to be an end of the universe and mankind as we know them in order to cleanse and begin again?

~

Of course, from the Buddhist viewpoint, not just from that of common sense, there is a beginning and there is an end. That is logical; that is law; that is nature. So whatever we call the Big Bang or such things, there is a process of evolution or a process of beginning. So there must be an end. In any case, I think the end won't come for several million years.

Now, pollution. As you know I come from Tibet. When we were in Tibet, we had no idea about pollution. Things were very clean! In fact, when I first came across pollution and heard people say that I could not drink the water, it was a surprise to me. Eventually our knowledge widened.

Now it is really a very serious issue. It is not a question of one nation or two nations, but of the survival and health of all of humanity. If we have a clear conscience about this problem and behave accordingly, it seems there is a way to at least lessen this problem. For example, two or three years ago when I was in Stockholm beside the big river, some of my friends told me that 10 years previously there had been no fish in the river because the water was so polluted. Around the time of my visit some fish had

~

begun to appear because of the control of pollution. So this shows that there is the possibility of improving things.

Killing and situations like Bosnia are immediately striking to our minds. Yet pollution and other environmental problems lack this kind of striking appearance. Gradually, month by month, year by year, things become worse and worse. By the time a problem becomes very obvious it may be too late. Therefore I think it is a very serious matter. I am quite encouraged that in many places people are clearly concerned, and even some political parties have been set up based on the ideology and policy of environmental protection. I think this is a very healthy development. So there is hope.

What suggestions can you offer to overcome social institutions, such as the news, entertainment, and media, which seem constantly to promote negative attitudes and emotions – the opposite of what you advocate?

~

That is true. I often express my concern at that. However, I think, as we discussed, much depends on our own mental attitude. When we look at these negative things – killing, sex, or that kind of thing – if we look at them from another angle, that is also useful. Sometimes you can use these scenes of violence, sex, and so forth in a more positive way, so that, by being mindful of the effect and destructive nature of these various human emotions, you can use this particular viewing as a reminder of their destructive nature. While images of sex and violence may be somewhat exciting initially, if you look further you can see no benefit.

~

Of course, I have another opinion of the media, I think especially in the West. In a country like India, killing and murder are often shown on television, but the sexual things are more censored. But if you compare killing and sex, sex is much better! If we pretend that it is not a part of human life, that is also not good, is it?

Anyway, I think it is equally important to make a clear presentation to the human mind of the other, good, human qualities, and I think that this is lacking. We only show the negative side – killing, sex, and all these things

~

– but the other side, the human acts of compassion, are not shown.

Now, for example, in Washington I visited the museum of the Holocaust. When I went there, after seeing all these things, I was reminded of both qualities of human beings. On the one side there was Nazi Germany's torture, killing, and extermination of the Jewish people – horrible and very sad. It reminds me how bad or awful it is if human intelligence is guided or motivated by hatred. But at the same time, another side showed those people who sacrificed their own lives in order to protect Jewish people. So that also shows the human good quality, to risk even their own lives to save unfortunate people. In that way, I think it was quite balanced. If we let hatred guide us then we can be so cruel and so destructive. But on the other hand, if we promote good human qualities, then wonderful actions and marvelous things can happen. Likewise, the media should show both sides. That is what I always feel.

~

Your Holiness, racism, bigotry and human folly seem to be on the increase. To what negative factors do you ascribe this? What positive factors can combat this trend?

~

~

I think they largely depend on education. I feel that the more correct information and the more awareness and contact you have, the better. Of course, you also have to adopt an open mind. After all, you are just one human being out of five billion and one individual's future depends very much on others. Part of the problem I see is a lack of awareness of other cultures and the existence of other communities, and also a lack of understanding of the nature or reality of modern existence. If it were possible to gain complete satisfaction and fulfilment by being totally independent within one's own culture and one's own community – to be totally

~

independent and unrelated to other communities around the world – then perhaps one could argue that there were grounds for subscribing to these misconceptions like bigotry and racism. But this is not the case. The reality of the existence of other cultures and other communities cannot be ignored. Moreover, the nature of modern existence is such that the well-being, happiness and success of one's own community are very connected with the well-being and interests of other communities and other societies. In such a complex modern world there is no room for bigotry and racism.

Now according to my own experience, there is no doubt that Buddhism is the most suitable religion for me. But this does not mean that Buddhism is best for everyone. Each individual has a different mental disposition and therefore for some people a particular religion is more suitable or more effective than others. So if I respect each individual's right, then I must respect or accept the value of these different religions because they work for millions of other people.

When I was in Tibet I had little information, through books or from personal contact, about

~

the nature and value of other traditions. Since I've become a refugee, I have had more opportunity to have closer contact with other traditions, mainly through individuals, and I have gained a much deeper understanding of their value. As a result, my attitude now is that each one is a valid religion. Of course, even from the philosophical viewpoint, I still believe that Buddhist philosophy is more sophisticated, that it has more variety or is more vast, but all other religions still have tremendous benefits or great potential. So on both bases, I think my attitude towards other religions is greatly changed. Today, wherever I go and whenever I

~

meet someone who follows a different religion, I deeply admire their practice and I very sincerely respect their tradition.

~

Is it possible for an ordinary person to transform his or her fear and despair? How *can we do this?*

Oh, yes, it is very possible. For example, when I was young I was always afraid of dark rooms. As time went by, the fear went. Also, with regard to meeting people, the more your mind is closed, the greater the possibility of developing fear or feeling uncomfortable. The more open you are, the less uncomfortable you will feel. That is my experience. If I meet anyone, whether a great man, a beggar, or just an ordinary person, to me there is no difference. The most important thing is to smile and to show a genuine human face. Different religions, different cultures, different languages, different races – these are not important. Educated or uneducated, rich or poor, there is no difference. When I open my heart and open my mind, I consider people just like old friends. This is very useful. On the basis of that kind of attitude, if the situation is something different then I have the freedom to act according to the circumstances. But at the beginning, from my side, I must create the ground. Then often there is a positive response from the human level. So I think fear is one thing to clear away.

Also, in the individual's mind there are many hopes. If one hope fails, it does not mean that all hopes fail. I have met some people who tend to feel completely overwhelmed and who become desperate when they are not able to fulfill one of their hopes. But I believe that the human mind is very complex. We have so many different types of hopes and fears that it is quite dangerous to invest everything on one particular hope, so that when that hope is not fulfilled we are totally overwhelmed. That is a bit too dangerous.

Your Holiness, in this country there has been a move away from religion in recent years. At the same time, there has been an increased interest in various forms of self-development. Is religion still an appropriate path in the modern world?

It is definitely relevant in the modern world. But perhaps I should clarify this. Many years have passed since various religious traditions started, so certain aspects are, I think, perhaps out of date. But this does not mean that religion as a whole is irrelevant in modern times. Therefore, it is important to look at the essence of the different religions, including Buddhism. Human beings, no matter whether today's or those of 100, 1,000, 4,000 or 5,000 years ago, are basically the same. Of course, a lot of the cultures and the ways of life have changed, but still we have the same kind of human being. So therefore, the basic human problems and suffering – such as death, old age, disease, fighting and all these things – are still there. I don't know what kind of shape humans will be in after 10,000 years or 100,000 years; nobody knows. But at least over the last few thousand years, they have, I think, kept basically the same nature.

So I think the various different religions actually deal with basic human suffering and problems. On that level, because human nature and suffering have remained the same, the religions are still very relevant. On the other hand, certain ceremonial aspects and so on have

~

changed. In India, during the feudal system or the reign of kings, the way of practice was very much influenced by those circumstances. But that has changed and, I think, has to change further.

As far as Buddhism is concerned, it of course not only deals with this life but with other more mysterious aspects. Unless, just as modernization is taking place in our world, a similar type of modernization is taking place in other realms of existence, I think Buddhism will retain its relevance and appropriateness, not only to our modern world, because many

~

of the fundamental problems of human existence still remain, but also because it addresses issues which are related to other mysterious forms of existence. I always believe that the modern change is just a surface change and that deep down we are the same. Last year at the border between Austria and Italy, they recovered an old body. If we were to suppose that the person was alive, I think we could still communicate with him. Yet the body is about 4,000 years old. Of course, that person would have a different culture and maybe a slightly different way of expression, but basically we could still communicate.

Could Your Holiness speak about interpersonal relationships in accordance with personal karma? How does one understand the difference between tolerance and stupidity?

~

True tolerance is a stand or a response an individual adopts in relation to a particular incident, or toward another person or event, when the individual has the ability to act in a contrary manner. As a result of one's considerations, taking into account many factors and so on, the individual decides against taking negative action, and this is true tolerance. This is quite different from a situation in which an individual has no capacity whatsoever to take such a strong countermeasure. Then he or she is in a helpless position, so can't do otherwise. The difference between the two is in fact quite clearly pointed out in

~

one of the Buddhist texts known as *Compendium of Deeds* by the Indian master Shantideva. So my tolerance toward the Chinese is actually quite open to question – is it really genuine tolerance or not?!

~

How may one overcome fear or fearfulness as a habitual state of mind, especially when there is no apparent cause?

~

I think that the kind of outlook you have and the way you think makes a big difference. Often we find ourselves being hit by a sudden thought or feeling, such as fear, which, if we leave to itself, or, in other words, give in to without paying much attention, can begin to work in its own cause and begin to affect us. It is crucial that when such things arise one must apply one's faculty of reasoning so that one does not fall under the sway of these thoughts and feelings. Of course, if there is sufficient reason to fear, then fear is good! Fear creates preventive measures, so that's good. Yet if there is no basis for fear, then when you meditate analytically the fear will be reduced. That's the proper way.

~

Can compassion arise spontaneously after one has developed direct intuitive insight?

~

I think it depends very much upon one's own spiritual orientation and the basic motivation. It is possible for certain practitioners who have developed familiarity with various principles of the path, altruism, and so forth. As the individual gains greater insight into the nature of reality, the greater the power of his or her compassion and altruism will be, because he or she will then see that sentient beings revolve in the cycle of existence due to ignorance of the nature of reality. Such practitioners, when they gain very deep insight into the nature of reality, will also realize the possibility of a way out from that state of suffering.

~

Once you have that realization, then your compassion toward sentient beings will be greater because then you will realize their fate – although they can get out, they are still caught in the cycle.

But simply because one has gained a certain degree of insight into the nature of reality does not guarantee an automatic spontaneous experience of compassion. This is because one's insight into the nature of reality can be motivated by an altruistic wish to help other sentient beings or it can be induced by a motivation primarily concerned with one's own

~

interest of attaining liberation from cyclic existence. So simply by generating insight into the nature of reality on its own cannot really lead to genuine compassion; you need some additional conditions.

~

Are there examples of the positive expression of anger based on compassion and self-understanding?

Yes, it is possible to have circumstances in which the basic motivation can be compassionate, but the immediate catalyst or motivating factor can be anger, which is a very strong force of mind.

Your Holiness, how can I stay in touch with my emotions without being afraid? I often control my feelings so much that I am closed off and unable to love.

When I talk about love and compassion, I make distinctions between the ordinary sense of love and what I mean by love. What I mean by love can arise on the basis of a clear recognition of the existence of the other person, and a genuine respect for the wellbeing and rights of others. However, love based on strong attachment toward one's close ones is, from the point of view of religious practice, something that has to be ultimately purified. A certain degree of detachment must be developed.

I think that perhaps at the beginning level you may find some kind of loneliness. Actually, that is one of the aims of the lives of monks and nuns. While in one way that sort of life may seem a bit colorless or unattractive, in another way it is more colorful. In reality, I think the one form of happiness has too much fluctuation, so I think in the long run the other type, although less dramatic, is something steady. In the long run I think that it is much more comfortable! So that is one consolation for monks and nuns!

If someone feels in the depths of despair and, in a very deep depression, lies at night wanting to die, what is your advice to help that person become more stable and positive?

~

It is very difficult if it is someone who has no background or practice. Then I really don't know what to advise. But if it is someone who has some experience or practice of some other religion, and if he or she has some experience of Buddhist practice, then it is helpful to think about Buddha Nature and about the potential of the human body and the human brain. It is also helpful to read the stories of great practitioners of the past, whose lives illustrate the hardships that people have gone through. For instance, in some cases these great masters were people who had previously had almost no education or people who were depressed and lacked facilities and so forth. But as a result of their determination and confidence in their own potential, they were eventually able to attain high realizations. One must also bear in mind that being depressed and losing hope will never really help to correct the situation.

Your Holiness, in trying to be a compassionate human being, how responsible should we feel? What should you do if you find someone emotionally dependent on your compassion? Is it compassionate to hurt someone if you think it is the best in the long run?

I think you should keep in mind compassion with wisdom. It is very important to utilize one's faculty of intelligence to judge the long-term and short-term consequences of one's actions.

I can understand how my own mind and actions can affect my own causes and conditions. Can they also affect world conditions like hunger, poverty, and other great sufferings of beings everywhere? How?

~

Sometimes we feel that one individual's action is very insignificant. Then we think, of course, that effects should come from channeling or from a unifying movement. But the movement of the society, community or group of people means joining individuals. Society means a collection of individuals, so the initiative must come from individuals. Unless each individual develops a sense of responsibility, the whole community cannot move. So therefore it is very essential that we should not feel that individual effort is meaningless – you should not feel that way. We should make an effort.

Words of inspiration from one of the world's most beloved spiritual leaders

His Holiness the Dalai Lama, the exiled spiritual leader of the Tibetan people, offers simple, practical advice on how we can bring more love and compassion into our lives. With his down-to-earth approach, he shows us how to truly accept others and how we can transform disturbing emotions, such as anger, into love, joy and peace of mind.

www.harpercollins.co.uk
www.harpercollins.co.in

Spirituality/Gift

www.thorsons.com

₹ 199

UK £5.99

ISBN 978-0-00-743524-1

00199

9 780007 435241

Thorsons
Directions for Life

FOR SALE IN THE INDIAN SUBCONTINENT ONLY